Seasons of Hope

Frank Bice

www.cranwellfoundation.com

Published by BookLocker.com, Inc., St Petersburg, Florida.

Printed on acid-free paper.

BookLocker.com, Inc.
2016

First edition

This book is dedicated to
Coach Thomas J. Sheehy III

Contents

Chapter I:
The Greatest Lacrosse Player in the World

Many years ago, I was the boys' junior varsity lacrosse coach at Saint Mary's in Manhasset, Long Island. On that J.V. team were up and coming stars, such as Billy Bergin, John Farrell, George Garcia, Chris Zenobio, and Steve Sombrotto. I'll never forget what happened this one season. Every day I would drive my van to the field for practice.

Almost every day, before I would get out of my van, a kid named Dave would approach the driver's side window and say, "I made a big mistake, I'm playing baseball, but I know I should be playing lacrosse."

Dave was a sophomore at Saint Mary's at the time and almost every day it was the same routine.

He would approach the van and say, "I know I should be playing lacrosse, but I'm playing baseball and it's killing me."

Finally one day I said, "Dave, what's going on in your life?"

Dave said, "My parents are going through a divorce and I don't know what to do. My dad was a baseball star and used to coach me in baseball. I've been playing baseball to try and help my parents' marriage, but I can't do it. I know I should be playing lacrosse." So I told Dave that I was going to be coaching summer league lacrosse at Manhasset High School and that he should come out.

Dave said, "Don't worry, I'm definitely coming out for summer league."

When summer league began, Dave came out with all of his equipment. He had a defenseman's stick and was really aggressive. Dave was over six feet tall, a natural lefty, fast, and a really good athlete. After we played a few summer league games, Dave gave me a list of five, Division I, college coaches that he wanted me to write to tell them that he needed a full scholarship for lacrosse.

I said, "Dave, you haven't even played in a varsity game yet, I can't write to these coaches."

Dave said, "Don't worry, I know I can do this, please just write the letters."

Dave, to his credit and because of his belief in himself, wouldn't take 'No' for an answer. Dave started calling me asking if I had written to the five coaches. Dave even showed up at my house one day looking for the letters. Finally, I wrote the letters. I heard back from only one college coach who said that we should wait and see how Dave did at the varsity level.

Dave took all the pain and heartache in his life and he took a step back. He looked at himself and he realized that he had a gift that no one else realized he had. Dave dropped everything else except for lacrosse. You never saw this kid without his lacrosse stick in his hands. Everyday he ran sprints and would do 'one on ones,' challenging anyone he could find to try and beat him to the cage. He focused on becoming the best lacrosse player he could possibly become. In Dave's junior year he made varsity and wound up starting. Dave started to dominate. After Dave's junior year, he made the Long Island Empire State Team. This is an incredible lacrosse team comprised of high school All-Stars who play against other All-Star select teams from all over New York State. Dave also attended every lacrosse camp that time would allow. In his senior year in high school Dave was incredible. Playing alongside goalie, Paul Schimoler,* Saint Mary's beat Saint Anthony's and Chaminade to win the Catholic School Championship.

Dave made High School All-American and earned a full scholarship to Johns Hopkins. At Hopkins, Dave's freshman year he got sick and he couldn't play for most of the season. His sophomore year he came back and made 1st Team All-American and his team won the National Championship. As a junior, Dave made 1st Team All-American. As a senior, Dave made 1st Team All-American and he was named Player of the Year in Division I college lacrosse. As a defenseman, being named Player of the Year is almost impossible. That award usually goes to a really high scorer (an attackman or a middy) it never goes to a defenseman. Dave, as a defenseman, was named Player of the Year in college lacrosse! At the same time that Dave was playing lacrosse, the Gait brothers were playing at Syracuse, twin brothers who were incredible. Dave was named Player of the Year above the Gait brothers. That is how amazing Dave was. After college, Dave kept on playing. He went on to make the United States Lacrosse Team twice. In the World Games in Australia, the United States defeated Canada, and Dave was named the Most Valuable Player of the World Games.

So here we are, just a few years earlier, this kid Dave would walk up to my van every day and say, "I'm playing baseball but I know I should be playing lacrosse." Then he is named the number one lacrosse player on the planet Earth. So what is the message for you and for me? All of us have a gift. All of us go through tough times. Do we have the strength, courage, and vision to take a step back and really look at our lives? Do we thank God for the unique gift that we have? Then do we go for it? That is exactly what

Dave did and he serves as a role model for all of us. What do we do with our frustration and our pain? Do we take the energy that we have as a result of our frustration and do we channel it into something incredibly positive? Dave did another really smart thing - **he asked for help**. Now, honestly, I contributed nothing to this kid's success in lacrosse. He did it all on his own. He found many excellent coaches and mentors along the way. I only coached him during that summer league. Dave did it all on his own. He focused on one thing and he went for it! All of us have a unique gift that we can do better than anyone else in the world. Our gift might be in sports and it might not be - it might be in art, music, writing or something academic. Your gift might be in business. Some of you guys might be rainmakers - you know what that means - people who know how to make a lot of money. Who knows? You might be a great coach or counselor. It's up to you to discover your unique gift and then go for it.

Dave did something else that was really smart. He didn't try to escape from his pain by using drugs or alcohol. The way all human beings grow is by dealing with challenges, working through them, and this is what makes us stronger. This is called the maturing cycle. When we are in high school and we get involved in drugs or alcohol, every time we escape from reality, we stop the maturing process. When we deal with daily challenges we get stronger. If we escape from reality through drugs or alcohol, over time what happens is when we become adults, in our hearts we are really like 14 or 15 year old kids because we have broken that maturing cycle. Dave did not make that choice. When his parents were going through their divorce, Dave took all of his pain and frustration and channeled into something incredibly positive, becoming the best lacrosse player he could become.

Today Dave Pietramala is the Head Lacrosse Coach at Johns Hopkins University. Dave has won two National Championships as the Head Coach. He has been voted Coach of the Year (at Cornell and Hopkins) and has the record for the most wins of any coach in the history of Johns Hopkins. Dave is considered by many to be the greatest defenseman in the history of lacrosse.

Paul Schimoler would become a four-time All-American at Cornell. Paul was Ivy Rookie of the Year as a freshman and Ivy Player of the Year as a senior. He played on two USA teams with Dave.

Chapter II:
Be True to Yourself

I can remember going up for early football practice when I was a freshman at Siena College, in Loudonville, NY. It was a hot August afternoon. I moved into my dorm room and met another freshman football player who had just moved in across the hall. Patrick Archer, or 'Arch,' was a big, strong, very quiet linebacker from upstate New York. When practice began, Arch looked pretty talented, but his shyness almost dictated the way he was perceived as a player. Arch was so shy and unassuming that no one noticed how good he really was. It wasn't until one of the last games of the season, when we were winning by a large margin, that the coaches finally put Arch in the game as an inside linebacker. I can remember when their quarterback handed the ball off to the halfback. He tried to run the ball up the middle of the field. Arch came up and hit the halfback so hard that he was knocked unconscious. There was dead silence. We all just stared in disbelief.

I said to myself, "My God, did I just see that?" All of a sudden we all realized that Arch was an awesome football player!

Needless to say, Arch started in every football game after that. In the years ahead he went on to make NCFA (National Collegiate Football Association) All-American.

After the football games in college, there would always be a big party on campus where everyone would go crazy. Arch never smoked or drank any alcohol. When he did show up at a party, Arch would be wearing a pair of jeans and an old flannel shirt. He would hang out with his hands in his pockets and just be true to himself. Before long, Arch became the most respected football player in the college. Everyone began to recognize that he spoke with his actions and not his words.

Arch and I were in the same English class our freshman year as well. Toward the end of the semester, we were assigned a ten-page paper that represented a pretty big part of our final grade. I figured that Arch would definitely need my help. I thought of myself as a fairly good writer so I asked Arch if he wanted me to help him write his paper. In his usual shy manner, he said that he thought he'd be okay writing it on his own. When we got the papers back, Arch got an 'A' and I got a 'C.'

Arch was not only a great football player, he went on to become a straight 'A' student as well. So much for needing my help! Through our years together in college, Arch and I became good friends. In his own quiet way, he became the leader of the team, the most popular football player, and the most respected. Ultimately, Arch was accepted into the Siena / Manhattan College Engineering Program. Today Arch is happily married, has several children, and is a very successful engineer.

Chapter III:
My Greatest Coach

I grew up in Manhasset, Long Island, and had a very happy childhood. I started playing football, basketball, and lacrosse in first grade. I was small, but I loved playing sports. The athletes I remember were the Coughlin Brothers, two sets of Driscoll Brothers, two sets of Farrell Brothers, the Denihan Brothers and Cousins, the Iskyan Brothers, the Kelly Brothers, the Sullivan Brothers, the Ryan Brothers, Brian Coen, the Smith Brothers, the Boylan Brothers, Tommy Adams, Joe LoLordo, the Beaudette Brothers, the Vosburgh Brothers, two sets of Gallo Brothers and Cousins, the Walker Brothers, the Johnston Brothers, the Judge Brothers, Dave Saunders, the Petracca Brothers, the Fierro Brothers, the Goulding Brothers, the Charbonneau Brothers, Guy Vitacco, the Maher Brothers, Charlie Cona, the LaPlaca Brothers, the Edmonds Brothers, the Molloy Brothers, Neil Brugal, Greg Barber, the Schultheis Brothers, Bill Geoghan, the Geiger Brothers, Kevin Cosgrove, Andy Ruggiero, Rob

Serling, Tim Lyons, the Valentine Brothers, Jim Murray, the Cuneo Brothers, the Baugher Brothers, Rich McAleese, John Prager, the Thomas Brothers, the Costello Brothers, the Furlong Brothers, Mark Sauvigne, the deVenoge Brothers, the Miller Brothers, Bob 'Hondo' Hendrickson, John Griffin, the Eckerson Brothers, the Falino Brothers, the Gleason Brothers, Joe Scott, the Brady Brothers, the Greene Brothers, Pete Bartlett, Chip Curtis, the Fitzsimons Brothers, the Wright Brothers, the Attia Twins, Ken Smerk, the Galvin Brothers, Mike Harris, Bruce Miller, the Fitzpatrick Brothers, the Barrett Brothers, the Walsh Brothers, Stauch Kushay, Jed Grennan, the Connolly Brothers, the Gately Brothers, Tom Nicosia, John Hill, Ray Randall, Marshall Tally, Chris Mehring, Bill McIntosh, Peter Chapdelaine, the Welsh Brothers, the Murphy Brothers, the Hone Brothers, two sets of Barry Brothers, the Conway Brothers, the Gahan Brothers, Barney Fields, Chris Corin, Vin Ieradi, the Crowley Brothers, the O'Connor Brothers, the Kenlon Brothers, Peter Locker, the Jagenberg Brothers, the Cimperman Brothers, Pete Bartley, John Idol, the O'Connell Brothers, the Coleman Brothers, the Gordon Brothers, the Beil Brothers, the Daly Brothers, the Malhame

Brothers, the Meade Brothers, two sets of Shea Brothers, the Meehan Brothers, the Connors Brothers, the Morrison Brothers, Chuck McCarthy, the Modica Brothers, the Berger Brothers, Jim McDonald, the Finnerty Brothers, Jim Hetherington, Jim Santoro, Tom Emma, Gordon Farkouh, Joe Morgan, Jim LaRocca, the Maguire Brothers, the Buhr Brothers, J.B. Meyer, the Magee Brothers, John Gula, Jimmy Power, Jerry Foerst, Bill Felton, the Cary Brothers, Timmy McCarthy, Robert Bollen, the Endres Brothers, the Leahy Brothers, Ron Petronella, the Grace Brothers, the Hannan Brothers, Rick Whipple, Chip Faulkner, the Holohan Brothers, Jay Ernst, the Petrie Brothers, the Larigan Brothers, Bob Marusi, the Powers Brothers, Tommy Andromedis, Joey Lynch, the Jennings Brothers, the Caldwell Brothers, the Stapleton Brothers, Peter Bradley, the Finnigan Brothers, the Bauer Brothers, Rick Andriano, the Rohn Brothers, the Crowell Brothers, the Lala Brothers, the Doran Brothers, the Purchase Brothers, Bob Anastasia, the Kucich Brothers, the Carlstrom Brothers, the Kelleher Brothers, the Stork Brothers, the Mahon Brothers, the Conroy Brothers, the Zazinski Brothers, the Smykowski Brothers, Brian Barolo, the Chikowski Brothers, Joe Moreman, the Burke Brothers, the Pegno Brothers, the Cullen Brothers, Dan Brown, Rob Gross, D.D. Skinner, the Monohan Brothers, the Higgens Brothers, the Haggarty Brothers, Gerard McQueeney, the Devereaux Brothers, the Snodgrass Brothers, the Brennan Brothers, Gary Burnes, the Thomas Brothers, the McLaughlin Brothers, Brian Byrnes, Mel McLaughlin, the Owens Brothers, the Kiess Twins, the Wilhouski Brothers, Joe Janek, Joe Gendusa, Kent Eppley, Matt Levine, the Rule Brothers, Peter Cordrey, the Erickson Brothers, the Williams Brothers, the Cerick Brothers, the Goettelmann Brothers, the Barnard Brothers, the Ross Brothers, Benji Green, the Brogan Brothers, the Cox Brothers, the Viscardi Brothers, John Kiggins, the Benincasa Brothers, the Collins Brothers, the McCooey Brothers, the Cronin Brothers, the Tunney Brothers, Dan Amoruso, Bobby Lubbers, the Bitter Brothers, Todd Dodge, the Glynn Brothers, the Oakes Brothers, the O'Malley Brothers, the Moore Brothers, the Johnson Brothers, the Keyloun Brothers, Ray Kane, Ken Weigand, the Lawrence Brothers, Tim Rooney, and the Kaufman Brothers.

I started to understand at an early age that if my coach believed in me, I could perform on a much higher level. I grew up in a single-parent household with a great mom, an awesome older brother, C.J., and terrific sisters, Teri, Peggy, and Kitty. C.J. was among the top horseback riders in the country and strong as an ox. C.J. and I would have endless baseball catches in our backyard. He was tough as nails and a great brother. With the foundation built by C.J., my coaches would become my father figures.

When it was time for me to go to high school, my mom believed it would be in my best interest to go away to boarding school. It turned out to be the best thing for me. I attended Cranwell in Lenox, MA. Among the great coaches I had at Cranwell were Buddy Pellerin and Tom Sheehy.

Coach Pellerin, the Head Football Coach, was all heart and full of passion for the game. Freshman year, I was too small for football and played soccer. As a sophomore, I barely made his football team. Among his great players were Mark Finn, Spike McQuail, Bob Froehlich, the Hatton Brothers, Sal Alessi, Dennis

17

'Rocky' McCarthy, Bill 'Whitey' Felton, Quentin Bradley, Rick McGrath, Dan Keegan, Chuck McGinnis, Bill Frazier, John O'Brien, Gerry Barr, Chris McInerney, Willie Rynn, Steve Gorman, Kevin Blough, Al Bianchi, Ron Snyder, Greg 'Howard' Cary, Larry McMahon, Rocky Campbell, Brian Lemieux, Steve Shay, Stanley Iglehart, Van Ferguson, Steve Ziegler, and Pat Morris.

Coach Pellerine orchestrated the upset of the century by beating Cheshire Academy. Linebacker, Gerry Barr, made the game-saving tackle by grabbing the Cheshire halfback's ponytail and stopping a touchdown. When Cranwell defeated Cheshire, the sportswriter from the *Berkshire Eagle* reported that it was the best football game he had ever witnessed. Captain Mark Finn would go on to play linebacker for the University of Miami. Kicker, Sal Alessi, made four separate All-American teams.

For those of us at Cranwell, Coach Pellerine will be remembered as one of the greatest football coaches ever. Throughout the state of Massachusetts, Coach Pellerine is known as a great football coach, and as a star baseball player and coach. Today, Buddy Pellerin Baseball Field is located in Pittsfield, MA.

For me personally, during my freshman year, I met my greatest coach, Mr. Thomas J. Sheehy III. Coach Sheehy taught me to believe in myself. Without him, none of my other experiences in sports, and life, would have ever happened. To say he was a strong influence is an understatement. The truth is he saved my life. Coach became the father I never had. I had Coach Sheehy for junior varsity basketball and lacrosse.

As a freshman, I tried out for junior varsity basketball. I was the smallest kid in the whole school. I thought that I would make the team, but that I'd be sitting on the bench most of the season. Coach Sheehy made me his starting point guard and told me to run the offense. By my coach believing in me, my confidence went through the roof. As a sophomore, I wound up averaging seventeen points a game and was elected captain of the team.

In lacrosse, if junior varsity didn't have a game, we would all suit up for the varsity game. I can remember my freshman year we all suited up for the varsity game. We were playing against a weaker team. I had three goals in the first half. During the break we were all sitting on the grass eating oranges, drinking water, and feeling pretty good about ourselves. All of a sudden Coach starts pacing back and forth and he looks really mad. We all thought we were in trouble.

Unexpectedly, Coach Sheehy grabs me by the jersey with both of his hands, lifts me up over his head, and starts screaming, "He's hungry! He's hungry! Did you see how he went to the cage! He's hungry!"

When Coach first lifted me over his head, honestly, he scared me. Then I realized that the man I looked up to more than anyone else in the world was praising me in front of my teammates. That moment changed my life. After that, anytime I walked out on the field, or on the court, I always believed that I would dominate. Coach Sheehy taught me to believe in myself. That gift has carried me through more situations in life than I can possibly describe. Among the lacrosse players who benefitted from Coach Sheehy were Tom Vagt, Dave Cleary, Dennis McCarthy, the Brown Brothers, Chrissy Bovers, Greg Carey, Van Ferguson, the Moynagh Brothers, Bill Felton, the Giguere Brothers, the Abbruzzese Brothers, Rob Stork, Geoff Regan, Gerry Barr, Dave Keating, Tom Sheridan, Kelly McCormick, John Roche, Mike Livingstone, Steve Gorman, the Giblin Brothers, Chuck McGinnis, Chris O'Connor, John Feeney, Matt Fitzsimons, the Deblois Brothers, Peter O'Leary, Tom Griffin, and Dan Keegan.

So what made Coach Sheehy so great? He praised in public and disciplined in private. Unless the entire team was at fault, then he would discipline all of us together. For the most part, he praised in public, and corrected in private. One basketball game, I scored 21 points in the first three quarters and was held scoreless in the fourth. After the game, Coach just showed me the scorebook and pointed to the empty space representing my scoreless fourth quarter. No further discussion was necessary.

He treated us all as individuals. Coach Sheehy loved us. He was passionate about everything he did. He took his work seriously. He was creative more than he was competitive. Don't get me wrong. Coach loved winning more than most coaches. Even more than that, he was creative in his substitutions, strategy, and the way he handled us. If a player had behavioral issues, Coach spent quality time with the kid so that he felt understood and accepted. He also had a beautiful wife, Betsy, who made us great spaghetti dinners. He taught us to be humble winners and gracious losers. He taught us to compete against ourselves, not against our opponents.

If I lived for a million years and said, "Thank you," every day, I still wouldn't be able to thank Coach Sheehy enough for what he did for us. We would have run through a brick wall for this man. Coach really led us by who he was as a human being.

Chapter IV:
A New Life

What I'm about to describe in this chapter are events surrounding a serious injury that I sustained while in college. It's a little scary, but I promise that things have turned out so well that I consider myself to be the luckiest person in the world.

When I was in college I played both football and lacrosse. I loved both sports and was captain of both teams. In lacrosse I was a middy and in football I was a safety. In lacrosse we had a really good team. We went undefeated my sophomore year and won most of our games over a span of four seasons.

Our attack was incredible. Tom Baldwin, Steve O'Shea, and Tony Astorino, put together one of the highest scoring offenses in the country. I ran on the first or second midfield line, faced off, and played man-down. Through the years I had the honor of running with, or coaching after my injury, Marty Pietroforte,

John Lambert, Mike Baldwin, Bryan Coakley, John Owen, Peter Gregory, Kenny Carter, Jamie Moran, Mike Gagliardi, Chip Magner, Bob Young, Mark Windover, Steve Gerbes, Jack Rowan, Kenny Finnegan, Rich Tierney, Craig Curry, John Pavain, John Chase, Bill Morgan, Dick Pepper, Kevin Maguire, John Coyne, Chris Baldwin, Lance Liebler, Tom MacKay, Mark Stack, Paul Finnerty, Tom Doerfel, Tom Recne, Mike Dent, Jack McNulty, Donny Krause, and Joey Marotta. Our defense was anchored by Mike Sweeney, Ken Walsh, Brandon McCallion, Brian Ranagan, Bob Walsh, Mark Jenkins, Gary Chatnik, Gary Schamader, Jay Runac, Marty Stowe, Paul Esposito, Bill Redmond, Bob McLaughlin, Manny Rapkin, and Bob Hutchinson.

I came in first or second among my teammates in picking up ground balls every year. We played for legendary coach, Russ Ferris. Resembling the Marlboro Man, Coach Ferris was, and still is, one of the greatest influences in my life.

When we won a game he would say, "Wham bam by geebers, that's all she wrote."

Coach Ferris would call everyone, "Doctor." Coach's beautiful wife, Maureen, always brightened up the sidelines. After my freshman season, Coach Ferris said I was "170 pounds of heart."

In football I made NCFA 2nd Team All-American my junior and senior years. Our football team was not as strong as our lacrosse team. We had some talented players. Two of our receivers, Mark Goc and Terry Bouchard, had tryouts with the Dallas Cowboys. My teammates included Jeff Alexander, Mike Ehlers, Pat Archer, Bob Hutchinson, the Furman Brothers, James Lyles, Mark Morrison, Dan Canniff, Cosmo Crupi, Mark Windover, Manny Rapkin, Chuck Hoyt, Tim Lange, Tom Lamb, Mike McDermott, Terry 'Rence' Regan, Dennis Buckley, Mike Campbell, Steve McKenna, Mark Canary, Jim Manning, D.J. Panetta, Tim Roche, Tim Kissane, Gary Kolakowski , Marty Crotty, Hank Bauer, Ed Brewster, Rick Saulsbury, Ken Comerford, Willie Harmon, Greg Cummings, Bob Ciasulla, George Barna, Tom Metzold, Mike Gagliardi, Bob Hope, Bob Pape, Jim Salvatore, Greg Winters, Randy Miller, Steve Norris, Steve Phelps, Bob Diaz, Jim Tracey, Mark Keefe, Larry Zezima, Willie McCoy, Rob Karath, Tom Mannix, Rick

Johnson, Andrew Linehan, Sal Battaglia, Jim Toczydlowski, Mike Plunkett, Joe Iacabucci, Joe Wendth, and Paul Sausville.

Our football coach, Ken Ralston, was a great man, but not your typical motivator. He looked like Alfred Hitchcock in coaching attire. He was a portly gentleman, stoic, slow moving, with sleepy and distant eyes.

While annunciating every word, he would begin many of our halftime speeches in a soft, monotone voice saying, "Gentlemen, you are the scum of the earth." At which point linebacker, Manny Rapkin, would have to be physically restrained from attacking him!

Coach Ralston treated me like a son. He genuinely liked me. This was strange because when he wasn't calling us the scum of the earth or comparing us to horse manure, he was totally emotionless.

He used to say I was "the heart and soul of the defense." We won about half of our games.

During the fall of my senior year, I was having a pretty good season. I had three interceptions in the first two games, and in the third game I picked off a pass in the first quarter. We were playing at Saint John Fisher College in Rochester, NY. They had a great coach, Bob Bayer, and an awesome quarterback, Alan DeLisle. This kid had a cannon for an arm.

They kept on splitting two receivers wide to one side of the field. You call that formation, twins. It was a passing situation and we were in zone coverage. I was deep over the center of the field covering a receiver, when DeLisle completed a short pass to the tight end, Joe Catan, who started running for a touchdown. In an effort to make a saving tackle, I came up and hit Catan as hard as I could. The mistake I made was that I didn't get my head up in time and as our bodies collided, I broke my neck. As I lay on my back the field, all I knew was that I couldn't move and I couldn't feel anything. When the trainers and coaches came out on the field they called an ambulance.

A trainer named Jo-Ann knelt by my side. I said to her, "Joe-Ann, I'm paralyzed."

She just repeated, "You are going to be ok."

I also said to myself, "Don't panic."

When the ambulance arrived, they placed a board under my body and lifted me inside. A priest from Saint John Fisher rode with us to the hospital. During the ride, I was praying, Hail Mary's, as laud as I could.

Once inside the emergency room, the doctors and nurses unscrewed my facemask, removed my helmet, cut off my jersey and shoulder pads, took a series of x-rays, and explained that I had a spinal cord injury and that if I lived, I would never walk again. The priest then gave me the Anointing of the Sick. After that, I went to confession in front of all of the doctors and nurses. I figured if I was going to die, I was going with a clean slate! Next they shaved my head and drilled six screws into my skull to secure a 'halo' to stabilize my spine. I passed out from the pain.

I spent the next four weeks in traction at Strong Memorial Hospital. I was in a machine called a Stryker frame, which was kind of like a narrow bed. They strapped me down to keep my body completely straight. I had to face the ceiling for two hours and then they would turn the bed over and I'd face the floor for two hours. They rotated my body like that, every two hours for a month. During this time, my family and friends were great. They were almost always at my side. My friends were really funny. Mike Ehlers brought up a magic marker and wrote notes to the nurses on my body! Chris O'Brien brought up a fake hand that looked real and hid it under my sheet. When the nurse turned over my Stryker frame, the hand fell on the floor and the nurse screamed and ran out of the room!

When you have a spinal cord injury it's not the end of the world. There will be times in your life when all you can control is your attitude. When something really devastating happens to you, look at it as an opportunity to prove how great you can be by keeping a positive attitude. Now, when someone you know has a serious injury you should just show up. Just be there. My friends were great. They fooled around a lot. Be careful with this. The person who is suffering might not be in the mood to joke around and may not appreciate your good intentions. They will appreciate your being there. When in doubt, just show up.

What happens when you have a spinal cord injury? When you try to move your body, let's use your right foot as an example, your brain sends a message down through the nerves in your backbone (your spinal cord) to the nerves in your leg and you move your foot. When I try to move my right foot, the message goes from my brain to the point in my backbone where my nerves are damaged and the message stops there. It's like a broken, or cut, telephone or electrical wire. The message stops where the wire is not connected. My body is exactly the same as it was before my injury except that the communication is interrupted because of the injured nerves.

Coach Ralston was devastated by my injury. When he would come to see me in the hospital, he couldn't hide his pain. He was like a big Teddy Bear that had been left behind by a grown-up child. He looked sad, alone, and brokenhearted. His weakness revealed the depth of his love and it made me strong. Knowing that Coach Ralston loved me so much touched my heart.

Coach Ferris was a rock. He was strong, encouraging, and positive. Coach Bayer and his football players from Saint John Fisher were great. Joe Catan, the man I tackled when I was injured, was afraid to come see me. When he came to the hospital I assured him that it wasn't his fault. Fisher split-end, Joe Fina, took care of my family and friends, making sure they all had places to stay. Coach Bayer, Father Travado, Joe Catan, and Joe Fina were constant visitors at the hospital.

When I was in traction and my friends weren't around, I had a lot of time to pray. As a kid, my mom had taught us to trust God and to put our lives in His hands. My coaches had always taught me to give 100% and to leave it all on the field. I looked at my time in traction as an opportunity to really trust God, and I had no regrets because I really did leave it all on the field. One night, while I was praying, I made a deal with God.

I said, "Lord, I know my life has not been perfect. I know no one's life is perfect. And even if I didn't have this injury, my life was never going to be perfect anyway. If You will give me the grace to live the rest of my life with a positive attitude, I'll say 'Yes' to whatever You ask me to do." In other words, I surrendered.

When I finally got out of traction and was able to sit in a wheelchair, a nurse came in my room and asked me to visit a newly injured patient down the hall named, Patrick Kennedy. I said, 'Yes.' After I visited Patrick, I felt great. I learned that saying, 'Yes,' would usually lead to some type of service and that any type of service, in the right spirit, would set you free.

The next invaluable lesson that I learned while I was in the hospital was to pray, "Thank You, Jesus."

A priest from Saint Mary's in Manhasset would visit and pray, "Thank You, Jesus," in my ear over and over again. When he would leave, I would say it over and over again.

I believe that gratitude is the secret to life. I'm convinced that God can't resist a grateful heart. Whatever your religious background is, if you are constantly grateful the world will open up to you. So for my remaining time that I was in the hospital, I constantly focused on what I had to be grateful for in my life and I always said 'Yes' anytime anyone asked me to do any kind of service. I spent eight months in the hospital after my injury and I became excited about my new life. The revelation that equipped me for the years ahead was this: **service makes you powerful and gratitude makes you invincible.**

Chapter V:
Wheelchair Sports

While I was in the hospital, I met the coach of a wheelchair sports team called the New Jersey Wheelers.

When she asked me if I'd join their team, I said, 'Yes.' The next weekend I found myself in the middle of the football stadium at the University of Delaware with a shot put in my hand. I had joined the New Jersey Wheelers and I was competing against the national champion, Skip Wilkins, in the field events. The shot put is like a small metal bowling ball. It feels like it weighs a ton! I threw it as far as I could. It barely cleared my knee and landed about ten inches from my chair.

It almost fell on my lap and I thought, "Wow, that would have hurt!" Skip threw his shot put about thirty feet. I think he set a world record.

For the next event we had to throw the disk. The disk is like a small metal Frisbee. It should float through the air like a Frisbee. When I threw it, it went end over end and flopped on the grass. I think it covered a distance of about four feet. My opponent threw the disk about fifty feet. So I got crushed in the second event. The third competition was the club throw. The club is like a small bowling pin that is designed for guys to be able to throw who have paralysis in their fingers. I threw the club about five feet. Skip Wilkins threw it practically out of the stadium. I was soundly defeated in every event, but I was proud of myself for trying.

The next day they signed me up for the fifty-yard dash. I was in a sports wheelchair on the starting line next to five other guys in wheelchairs.

Then I heard, "Bang!" the gun went off! Everyone started flying down the track and my chair didn't move. One of my front wheels was jammed and eventually I started creeping along. A fifty-yard dash in a wheelchair should only take seconds to complete. It was taking me minutes to move down the track. My coach was walking next to me saying, "Frank, please, you don't have to finish the race. You're holding up the next event."

I said, "Coach, I started this race, I have to finish it!"

Now one of the guys I was racing against had fallen out of his chair and was unconscious on the track.

As I rolled by him, at first I felt sorry for him, but then I thought, "At least I might not come in last!" Well, believe it or not, they revived him, got him back in his chair, and he beat me at the finish line. At the end of the race, I was proud of myself for finishing, but a little embarrassed that it took me six minutes and forty seconds to go fifty yards. By the end of the weekend, I had learned a valuable lesson: sports would still be a big part of my life. Saying Yes' brought me back to a world that I loved.

Chapter VI:
Swimming

After spending eight months in the hospital, three months at Strong Memorial and five at the Rusk Institute, my family had generously made our house wheelchair accessible. My first night back home, I slept in a room downstairs. That morning when I woke up, something horrifying happened. I was looking into the faces of two of the Miller brothers. If you're from Manhasset, you probably know the Miller family. There are ten brothers and two sisters and these guys are nuts!

So I said, "Oh, hey guys, what's up?"

They replied, "We're here to take you swimming."

I asked, "Swimming? Have you guys noticed the wheelchair? I'm paralyzed. I can't go swimming."

They replied, "We don't care. Our Mom got you a waterskiing vest and you are going to go swimming in our grandparents' pool. Let's go!"

The next thing I know, I've got the vest on and I'm doing laps in their grandparents' pool. Everyday that summer, two of the Millers showed up and took me swimming. Believe me, it was the last thing I wanted to do, but it was the best thing for me. By the end of the summer, I could actually swim a mile. Every now and then, they would take me to Jones Beach or out to the Hamptons and they would carry me in the ocean. Once we got past where the waves were breaking, I could swim on my back. To be honest with you, I was never really that comfortable swimming in the ocean, but it was good for me.

One Saturday we drove out to the beach in the Hamptons. There had been a heavy storm the night before. When we arrived at the beach, the red flags were blowing in the wind and the waves were huge!

I was about to say 'No,' probably for the first time since my injury, but when I looked at Eugene Miller and Chris O'Brien, they said, "You're going in." O'B had me in a bear hug and Eug had my legs and as they carried me in the ocean. The waves were killing us. Finally, when we got past where the waves were breaking, I started to swim on my own. Next a rip tide got a hold of my body, and I was quickly pulled out to sea.

The ocean swells were huge. I was going way up and way down. I was about a half mile from shore and I was afraid, but then something terrifying happened. When I was on the top of one of those swells, I saw Eug, from a distance, had a look of fear in his eyes. I had known this kid my entire life. Never once had I ever seen a trace of fear in his face. When he looked afraid, I became petrified. I honestly thought that they were going to have to call the Coastguard to try and rescue me. Eventually, Eug swam out and got a hold of my foot, dragged me to shore, and we were all fine.

Chapter VII:
Teammates

When Cranwell closed in 1975 seventeen of us transferred to Canterbury in New Milford, CT. Coach Sheehy went to Tabor in Marion, MA. I missed Coach Sheehy, but in my senior year at Canterbury, I made the Western New England All Star Team in lacrosse and Coach Sheehy coached the Eastern All Stars. It was an honor to play against his team.

At Canterbury, my junior year I played lacrosse for Coach Charlie Huntington. Coach Huntington moved me from attack to midfield. He was a great coach who would become known for his incredible hockey teams.

My senior year I was captain of the lacrosse team and had the honor of playing for Coach Bill Fowler. Coach Fowler was a legendary football and lacrosse star at Hofstra. Paving the way for his brothers, Mike and Joe, and his sons, Billy and Jeff, the Fowler name is synonymous with greatness in the world of lacrosse.

With a pass and cut offense, Coach Fowler empowered us to reach our full potential. Coach Fowler stressed fundamentals and gave us the freedom to be creative at the same time. With his beautiful wife, Susan, Coach Fowler brought our program to another level. I could not have asked for better high school lacrosse coaches than Sheehy, Huntington, and Fowler. Coach Fowler would become one of the most important influences in my life. Without Coach Fowler, I would have never made All-New England my senior year. Coach Fowler made it possible for me, and so many other players, to be able to play in college. Today, I'm proud to say that Coach Fowler is one of my best friends.

Among those who benefitted from Coach Fowler were Rob 'Brillo' Santangelo, Roy Fugazy, the O'Brien Brothers, Peter Williams, Phil Curry, Gerry Phelan, Kevin McAvoy, Peter Tucker, Brian Murray, Rich Brancato, Tim Barry, Steve Kiernan, Glen Falk, Chip Ingrassi, Larry Fisher, Monty Clarke, Jim O'Meara Dave Glynn, Tom Burke, Tom Sheridan, Tom Ewing, and Mike Maugher.

My friends at Canterbury were great. After my injury, Mike Kiernan built me a standing frame to get me on my feet. Chris O'Brien made his apartment in Boston completely wheelchair accessible and was always at my side. Coach Fowler, Terry "Rence" Regan, Vinny Flynn, Garth Martin, Fish, Brillo, Greg Kiernan, Joe Viau, Tim Brown, Geoff Regan, George Malhame, and Eddie Perley were awesome.

When we were students at Canterbury, every winter we would head into New York City for the Gold and Silver Ball. This was a formal event that attracted prep school kids from all over New England. Our senior year, while most of us were scrambling to find a date, Rence decided to go alone. He rented a tuxedo, ordered the limo with us, and danced with our dates all night. Rence had more fun at the dance than the rest of us.

After we graduated from Canterbury, Rence and Vinny attended Syracuse. After three semesters at Syracuse, Rence decided to leave. So he came and lived with me, illegally, at Siena. Eventually, Rence was able to transfer into Siena and we played on the football team together. Before long, Rence became the most popular kid at our college. He had the prettiest girlfriend on campus named, Virginia. The day of my injury, I can't tell you what a huge consolation it was to have Rence on the team.

After months of rehabilitation and then spending the summer swimming with the Millers, I had to decide about going back to college. I only had one year to make up, but I didn't want to go back to Siena because I thought everyone would remember me the way I was before my injury, and now I was going back in a wheelchair. Coach Ralston and Coach Ferris encouraged me to come back and said that I could serve as an assistant coach on the football and lacrosse teams. A lot of my friends encouraged me to come back. The deciding factor was Rence.

Rence said that if I came back he would be my roommate, and that he would take care of everything.

So I said, 'Yes.' When I went back for my second senior year, everyday for nine months, Rence got me showered, dressed, helped me into my wheelchair, helped me go to the bathroom, helped me go to bed at night, pushed me to class, and got me to football and lacrosse practice. The way that Rence helped me, he made it so much fun, that we were laughing everyday for the entire year. Anyone who witnessed the way Rence helped me, would always have a smile on their face.

Rence gives us a classic example of how to be a great friend. If you have a friend, family member, or you know someone who needs help, just show up. Just be there. When you are called upon to serve, do it joyfully and make it fun. Make the person being served feel great. Never serve out of obligation. Make it a privilege and make it fun. When Rence, literally, carried me through my final year of college, he made me feel absolutely wonderful. That year Rence set me free. His spirit and enthusiasm set the whole college free. The year that I went back to college in a wheelchair was my best year of college. I loved it. All thanks to Rence. God obviously rewarded my good friend. Today Rence is very happily married to Virginia, they have six beautiful kids, and he is a very successful businessman. Be powerful and make service fun.

Chapter VIII
The Head Football Coach

Many years later, I was invited to go back and teach and coach at Canterbury. Amazingly, Coach Sheehy, my coach from Cranwell, became the headmaster at Canterbury. Now he hired me to be his teacher and coach. Feeling like the Prodigal Son, I was home again with my Father. Once again, my coach believed in me.

When I came back to Canterbury, I taught several classes, and coached football, basketball, and lacrosse. One of the major challenges I faced was becoming the head football coach. The team had a four-year winless streak and I was coaching the sport that I was playing when I had my injury. The kids on the football team were great. Among our players were Chris McManus, Paddy McCarthy, Matt Mulhern, Jim Northrup, Sean McCauley, John Duff, Steve Delany, Mark Cunningham, Atul Aneja, Owen Perkins, Anthony Dicarlo, Matt Michaud, Frank Radin, Keith Pio, Vin O'Connor, Mike

Mullady, Chris Smith, John Croyle, Mike Estroff, Brendan Wahlberg, Justin Smith, Dan Ferreira, Chris Seherr-Thoss, Ryan Pospisil, Bill Desmarais, Daryl Boston, Eric McMinn, Rahsaan Hunt, George Coville, Dan Tewaldi, Owen Perkins, Ed Federovich, Bill Hogan, John Constantine, Bill O'Shea, Chris Smith, Joe Quaranta, and James Dimino. My chair disappeared and we focused on turning around the program.

We started trying to achieve small victories. Our practices went really well. Every year the opening game was against Avon Old Farms, a powerhouse in Connecticut. During the week of the first game, I drove my van to Avon and found a farmer who agreed to let us do our pre-game warm-ups on his farm.

On the day of the opening game, we did our pre-game warm-ups on the farm, boarded the bus, and arrived at the game field thirty seconds before the opening kickoff. My players sprinted off of the bus and stormed the field. That momentum carried us for the first half. We got crushed in the second half.

We tried everything to break the losing streak. We had trick plays.

I taught them one play where the offensive line was positioned on the ball, the quarterback took his position behind the center, turned, and started walking toward our bench saying, "Wait a minute Coach, this play's never going to work!"

As soon as the quarterback said the word, "Work," the center would snap the ball back to the fullback and he'd run the ball up the middle of the field. When we tried running this play, the center snapped the ball over the fullback's head and we lost several yards.

We kept losing. I'll never forget the second to last game of the season. It was a home game against Westminster. It was freezing cold. We were being assaulted by hail, sleet, driving rain, and, not to mention, our opponent. Down 42:0 at halftime, we were frozen, banged up, and demoralized. During home games, my players would carry me down the field house steps for the halftime speech.

On this day, I can remember thinking, "What am I possibly going to say to these guys to make them want to go out and play the second half?" I decided to pull out all the stops. My kids were ready to quit.

I said to my players, "I'm proud of you because you haven't given up. The truth is, there is no way we are going to beat this team today. That's not the important thing. The important thing is for you to put on your helmets and go out there and finish what you started. Thirteen years ago, I walked onto a football field and never walked off. I lost. Everyday since then, I've put on my helmet and gone out there, knowing that I'll face huge challenges. The secret to life is putting on your helmet and fighting until your last breath. It's putting on your helmet, even if you know you are going to lose, and doing it because that's the promise you made to yourselves and your friends. The reason you play this game is because you love each other. Love is a decision. Because you love each other, you will be there to pick up each other, even when you are getting crushed. It's not about the scoreboard anymore. It's about standing up for each other and finishing what you started." We went out, held them scoreless in the second half, and we scored a few times. We finished the game. Then we lost the next game of the season. Now the school had a five-year winless streak.

The next season we were pretty strong, we won a few games, and turned things around. Behind the running of Frank Radin,* we even beat Westminster, the team that had pounded us on that bone-chilling day. Shortly after that, I went to graduate school at Yale. As I look back, I'm proud that we broke the five-year losing streak. I'm most proud of the team that had the courage to finish the game, on the day that we got crushed in the freezing rain.

Frank Radin would go onto become a 1st Team All-American in lacrosse at the University of Maryland.

Chapter IX:
"Coach, I Can't Find My Shoe!"

At Canterbury I coached the Boys' Junior Varsity Basketball team. I ran the same offense that Coach Sheehy had taught me at Cranwell. Sports were mandatory. Every kid had to play a sport every season. One year I had eighteen boys tryout for the team. These were great kids. Many were strong athletes, but not gifted basketball players. If the guys didn't make this team, they could play intramurals. I thought that six of the boys would gladly play intramurals. They'd have Wednesdays and weekends off and no away games, (which were usually halfway across New England!)

Among my J.V. players during my time at Canterbury were Kevin 'Classic' Conroy, also known as 'Cons, Tim McCarthy, the Sullivan Brothers, Herman Lee, Casey Kimma, Eric Dostie, Patrick Egan, Rahsaan Hunt, Justin Brynn, Owen Perkins, Chris 'Shack' Okelo, Gary Michael, Marcus Gaylord, Mark Lane, Sean McCauley, Brendan Wahlberg, Alex Soini, Tom

Custance, Mike Lamothe, Dan McCarthy, Dylan Crowley, Gavin Menu, Sean O'Dowd, Matt Sweeney, Bryan Bollen, and Mike Petrie.

At the next practice I called the eighteen players over and said, "I'm not making cuts this year. I need six of you guys to step down on your own and play intramurals. I'm not cutting anyone. I promise. Now let me see a show of hands. I need six of you to step down." Not one hand went up.

I said, "Fellas please, I need six of you to step down!" No one would quit. I kept all eighteen.

When the games started, we would have five guys on the court, and thirteen on the bench. My bench looked like the Russian Army! Invariably, we would be getting killed. We would be losing something like 90 to 20 and I'd call timeout.

I'd say, "If we keep them under 100 and we score 25, pizza in my apartment after the game." We would keep them under 100 and hit 25 at the buzzer and my eighteen lunatics would be running around the gym like they just won the N.B.A. Championship! The other teams didn't want to make eye contact with us because they thought we were crazy. I can't tell you how much money I spent on pizza that season.

For away games, my players would have to carry me on the bus. They practically killed me getting me on and off the bus. They would put my wheelchair below with the basketballs. One day we had an away game at Westminster and there were snow flurries beginning to fall during our ride up there. We lost something like 115 to 14 and the flurries turned into a blizzard. One of my players, Brendan Wahlberg, was pushing me in my wheelchair to the parking lot and neither one of us noticed where the curb ended and the parking lot began because of the snow. All of a sudden, my front wheels go off the curb and I fall out of my chair and I'm laying face down in the snow.

I was thinking, "It can't get any worse than this."

As I was lying there, one of my players, Alex Soini, comes running up to me and yells, "Coach, Coach, I can't find my shoe!"

My first thought was, "Wow, I'm going to kill you." Then I started to laugh because I realized how funny it was. He reminded me that we have to keep a sense of humor. Even though, he wasn't kidding, he really wanted me to help him find his shoe! We went 0 and 20 that season, but we had a lot of fun.

Chapter X:
Love Yourself

In the fall of 2007, I was invited to speak to the football team at Saint John Fisher College, the team I was playing against when I was injured so many years ago. I spoke to the team in their new stadium and then I went back to the field where I had my accident. It was a beautiful, sunny day, and I was sitting in my wheelchair on the exact spot where I had broken my neck twenty-seven years earlier.

I began to pray, "Thank You, Jesus," over and over again.

As I looked down on the grass, I had a conversation with myself, the twenty-one year old football player who, I envisioned, was lying there on the grass.

I said to him, "I love you so much, and I'm so proud of you. Thank you so much for giving everything you had and for leaving it all on the field."

And then I told him "I'm sorry I didn't love you the way I should have when I was your age."

When I was a kid, I spent so much time beating myself up with negative words and criticism that it was crazy. I didn't know that it was okay to love myself. Then, in my mind, the twenty-one year old football player looked up at me and said something that almost knocked me out of my chair.

He said to me, "Thank you for going ahead with your life. Thank you for staying involved with sports and for being the great man that you are."

And then he said something which changed my life, he said, "I don't care if you become the most successful person in the world or a skid-roe bum. I don't care. I will always love you and be there for you for the rest of your life." At that moment I realized that I am the luckiest person in the world.

As I rolled off the field, I prayed, "Thank You, Jesus," over and over again.

Through the years, I've had great highs and extreme challenges. After I left teaching and coaching at Canterbury, I graduated from Yale in 1996, and worked on Wall Street for fourteen years. I then taught and coached at Sacred Heart Academy in Hempstead, Long Island, for three years.

At Sacred Heart I had the honor of working with Deacon Jim and Marie Flannery, Mark Trolio, Andrea Grady, Peggyanne Shaw, Mary Jo Clarke, Mike Goetz, and Coach Morgan Molinari O'Connor. In class I enjoyed the wrestling matches between cousins, Kim Barry and Kathleen Kelly. It was scary when Kelly O'Krepkie and Kathleen Kelly would push me in the elevator and turn off the lights. It was equally scary when Brooke Williams slapped Cara Urbank. I got dizzy watching Elena Perez do laps around the auditorium while priests were hearing confessions. Ryann Coughlin-Roberti always brightened up my day.

Among our stars in the classroom, the court, or the field, were Kathleen Berkery, Kelly O'Krepkie, Nicole Carpenter, Jen Kiggins, Emily Sandford, the Labruna Sisters, Kaitlin Shanahan, Maria Rooney,

Rebecca Kinsley, Kelly Marsigliano, Paige Carter, Moira O'Connell, Liz Gomiela, Shannon Etts, the Biscardi Sisters, Sydney Carlino, the Malhame Sisters, the Harold Sisters, Sarah Morovich, Grace O'Connell, Caitlin McNamara, the Sheehan Sisters, Devon Denihan, the Mulhall Sisters, Sobrina Morasco, the Moran Sisters, Cara Urbank, Maggie Mahon, Kate Hegermiller, Shannon Atwell, and Emma Kenny. A gifted player with lighting speed, Shannon Atwell always managed to get wacked on the head! Emma Kenny liked to practice lacrosse in her loafers.

In 2014, Coach Sheehy invited me back, again, to be a faculty member at Canterbury. Perfectly illustrating the unconditional love of the Father in the Parable of the Prodigal Son, Coach was waiting for me. This past spring, we both served as assistant coaches with girls' varsity lacrosse. Forty-three years after Coach Sheehy first changed my life, miraculously, I was back on the field with Coach!

With instructions like, "Cut the cutters and fill the passing lanes!" Coach always said the right thing, at the right time, in the right way. He was just as intense and as great as he was on the field at Cranwell. The girls on the team loved Coach Sheehy. This being Coach Sheehy's retirement year, Coach and I were among those to whom the seniors dedicated the yearbook.

Coach Sheehy, Maeve Carroll, and I assisted Head Coach Lindsay Mulhern. Coach Mulhern had been a Division I star in college and won two World Cup Championships as the U.S. Under 19 Women's Lacrosse Head Coach. Lindsay's husband, Matt Mulhern '95, serves as our Director of Admissions. As a student at Canterbury, Matt led our hockey team to win the Division I Championship. While at Boston College, Matt won two Hockey East Championships, played in two Frozen Four Championships, and was a two-time All-Norton Team selection.

Among our great players on the Canterbury Girls Varsity Lacrosse Team were Hannah Krin, Sarah Bouwman, Lexi Rullo, the Martino Sisters, Emily Keating, Patsy Buckley, Sophie Menges, Sophia Poli, Julia DellaRusso, Aaliyah Biondo, Maddie Finnen, Jenna Joyal, Maddi Blauth, Reagan Bednar, Ali Goraci, Gabby

Vitelli, Sinead O'Donnell, Mary LaVigne, Christine Fromageot, Chesi Piccolo, Gigi Schullery, and Deb Cox.

If you get anything out of this book, the most important lesson is to learn to love yourself unconditionally. Just as Coach Sheehy taught me, repeatedly, to believe in myself, you need to believe in yourself. Say encouraging things to yourself and build up yourself. Even when you make a big mistake, you still need to love yourself. You can't expect anyone to be there for you if you are not willing to be there for yourself. Learn to love yourself!

Lessons to Remember

Just like Dave, who became the best lacrosse player in the world, when you are going through a tough time, take that energy and channel it into your unique gift. You have a unique gift, find out what it is. Especially when you are young, don't mess up the maturing cycle by using drugs or alcohol. Don't hang out with people who do use drugs or alcohol, you will get hurt. Find an adult you can trust and talk to them. We all need someone to talk to from time to time.

Say 'Yes' to service and make it fun. Just show up when someone is hurting. Be creative verses competitive. Be constantly grateful. If you experience a perceived failure and you remain grateful, something better will come along. When times are really tough, prove how great you can be by choosing to be positive. **Service makes you powerful, gratitude makes you invincible.** Be true to yourself. Love yourself. Put on your helmet every day and go out there and be proud of yourself for having the courage to enter the game.

** Special thanks to: Coach Tom Sheehy, Coach Buddy Pellerin, Coach Bill Fowler, Coach Steve Fernow, Coach Jack Gaudreau, Coach Peter O'Donnell, Coach Joe Fitzgerald, Coach Tim Biladeau, Coach Ron Kasuba, Coach Brian Meehan, Coach Tom Rooney, Coach Dan Sullivan, Coach Jules Viau, Coach John Hebert, Coach J.P. Mandler, Coach Don Robert, Coach Morgan Molinari O'Conner, Coach Dennis O'Brien, Coach Mike Goetz, Coach Kristen Schreiner, Coach Patrick Finn, Coach Chris Hopkins, Coach Maeve Carroll, Coach Lindsay Mulhern, Coach Shawna Altdorf, Coach Pete Crowley, Coach Tommy Adams, Coach Julius Picardi, Coach Kevin Cook, Coach George Bruns, Coach Bill Kirsch, Coach Rob Reddington, Coach Manny Rapkin, Coach Tom Taylor, Coach Jim Stone, Coach Paul Streaman, Coach Derek Richardson, Coach Ed Johannes, Coach Long Ding, Coach Jack Karpoe, Coach Don Robert, Coach Angelo Cona, Coach Paddy McCarthy, Coach Pete Cotier, Coach Tom Morris, Coach Max Bracero, Coach Charlie Vachris, Coaches Chris and Charlie Huntington, Coach Walter Burke, Coach Jim Sweeney, Coach Keith Rado, Coach Chris Roberts, Coach Sam Hargrove, Coaches Julio and Amy Omana, Coach Bill Olsen, Coach Dave Wilson, Coach Mark

Vanasse, Coach Fran Foley, Coach Lou Ventura, Coach Dave Pietramala, Coach Paul Schimoler, Coach Ken Ralston, Coach Walt Carswell, Coach Bob Bayer, Coach Dave Lucaroni, Coach Connor Wilson, Coach Marie Adams, Coach Carm Cozza, Coach Bob Estock, Coach Harvey Cohan, Coach Peter Van Dusen, Coach Dan O'Connell, Coach Tim Langton, Coach Luke Driscoll, Coach Tom Blake, Coach Brian Tunney, Coach Bruce Minerly, Coach Tim Welsh, Coach Bob O'Connell, Coach Mike Driscoll, Coach Dan Lane, Coach Jimmy Judge, Coach John Gagliardi, Coach Brian Kelly, Coach Pat Connolly, Coach Rick Buhr, Coach Dan Denihan, Coach Barbara Kiggins, Coach Ken Carter, Coach Roger Coleman, Coach Jack DuBois, Coach Gary Hearst, Coach Tom Burnes, Coach Steve Hart, Coach Tom Pillsworth, Coach Mark Jenkins, Coach John Svec, Coach Brian Brecht, Coach John Murphy, Coach Bryan Coakley, Coach Jay Ryan, Coach Jim Santoro, Coach Tim Cluess, Coach John Finneran, Coach Kevin Murray, Coach Pat Coleman, Coach John Kiggins, Coach/Father Mike Tedone, Coach Bob 'Meat' Murphy, Coach Tony Capozzoli, Coach Tore Barbaccia, Coaches Ed and Matt Sheerin, Coach Ed Colverd, Coach Cosmo DeLillo, Coach Bob Pomponio, Coach John Bransfield, Coach Gary

Chatnik, Coach Phil Ruggiero, Coach Homer Eckerson, Coach Charlie Morrison, Coach John Cardillo, Coach Joe Fields, Coach Frank Martocci, Coaches W. Harry and Harry L. Baugher, Coach Dick Widmeyer, Coach Tom Raleigh, Coach Rich Reichert, Coach Frank Coughlin, Coaches Arnold and Ronald Gallo, Uncle Tom at Pollywog, Coach Ed Cunningham, Coach Brogan, Coach Matt Panetta, Coach Pat Walsh, Coach Bob Rule, Coach Bill Cherry, Coach Allen Lowe, Coaches Bill, Eugene, Kevin, Dean, Patrick, Blake, Drew, Brady, and Ryan Miller, Coach Walter France, Coaches Ken Johnston Sr. and Jr., Coach/Brother Kenneth Robert, Coach Nick Colamarino and Coach Russ Ferris.